Wc

Discovering the God We Worship in 101 Ways

Worship the Lord with all your heart and enjoy Him forever

FireWorks International

Worship 101
Discovering the God We Worship in 101 Ways

Christopher Cunningham, Ph.D.

*Foreword by
Pastor Dan Backens*

FireWorks International
Virginia Beach, Virginia
www.fireworkstv.com

Worship 101:
Discovering the God We Worship in 101 Ways

Copyright © 2010
Written and compiled by
Christopher J. Cunningham, Ph.D.
All rights reserved.

No part of this book may be used or reproduced in any manner whatsoever without written permission of the publisher except in the case of brief quotations in articles and reviews.

Cover artwork & design: Jessica Miller
www.jroseart.blogspot.com

For information write:
FireWorks International,
2537 Belmont Stakes Drive,
Virginia Beach, VA 23456.
www.fireworkstv.com
757-966-0312

ISBN: 1451529279
EAN-13: 9781451529272.

Unless otherwise indicated, scripture taken from the New King James Version. Copyright © 1982 by Thomas Nelson, Inc. Used by permission. All rights reserved

Printed in the United States of America.

DEDICATION

To
The Holy Spirit

For energizing, strengthening, comforting and teaching me. You have taught me more about worship than anyone else could.

When I least expected it, You surprised me with Your awesome power and presence and revitalized my lukewarm Christian life.

You pointed me to the God that is a very personal being and who is interested in every area of my life. I am forever grateful.

Cover artwork & design: *Jessica Miller*
www.jroseart.blogspot.com

IN APPRECIATION

I wish to thank my beloved wife and ministry partner, Dahlia for her constant support, assistance, patience and emotional stability during the writing/compilation of this book. I am especially thankful for your meticulous editing and cross referencing.

To my sister-in-law Claudette Altman, your tremendous help in research, advice and encouragement are just what the doctor ordered. Without you, this project would have been twice as challenging. Thanks a million.

To Pauline Samuels, thanks for helping to keep the "little boat" afloat and for always encouraging me to write.

Thanks to our supporters at FireWorks International. It is through your prayers and gifts that we have been able to continue. Special thanks to Wes and Cynthia Burwell, our longtime and faithful partners. Also, to Amy Maloney, who helped with the typing and is always willing to volunteer at FireWorks International. To Jessica Miller, thanks for your professionalism with the cover artwork and design.

Thanks to my home church, *New Life Providence Church* in Virginia Beach, Virginia (particularly the *International Café Service*). To our dynamic Life Group (home Bible study group), especially Selina Simpkins and Annette Bowen; I enjoy worshiping the Lord with you and growing together. Your love for God always inspires me. Finally, thanks to my good friends Pastors Kevin Turpin, Tina Davis and Melvin McCleese for your encouragement, and to Senior Pastor Dan Backens for his spiritual guidance and support over the years.

CONTENTS
(Teaching Sections)

Foreword …………………..……………..	*xi*
Introduction ………………………………..	*xii*
Guide to Worship ………………………....	*11*
Emotions ……………………..……………	*23*
Ideas for Family Worship …………..…………	*35*
The Biblical Names for God ………..….....…...	*46*
What is Your Worship Ratio? …..………………	*57*
The First Commandment ………………….…..	*69*
Love Letter From God ………………………..	*81*
The Relevance of the Old Testament Names of God ………..………………..	*92*
Music & Worship ……………..………………	*103*
Final Words ……………………………............	*115*
Index ……...………………………………………	*116*

Worship 101

Discovering the God We Worship in 101 Ways

FOREWORD

One of the signs of revival is the restoration of the purity and passion of worship. It seems when the Spirit of the Lord woos His people to return to their first love that worship is always revitalized. Jesus said in John 4:23 *"But the hour is coming, and now is, when the true worshipers will worship the Father in spirit and truth; for the Father is seeking such to worship Him."* You and I live in the hour when God is deliberately seeking worshipers.

As Dr. Chris Cunningham's pastor, I know first hand that what he writes in *Worship 101* he lives out in his daily walk with God. He is a highly educated man but he has never yielded to the subtle snare of sophistication that domesticates worship but rather he has grown into a whole-hearted full-orbed worshiper of God. At his core, Chris is a revivalist.

The descriptions of God in his book and their accompanying Scriptural references will stimulate any heart to come alive in worship if you will ponder them in prayerful reflection. And like a wise shepherd who knows the ways of God firsthand, Dr. Chris will guide you with his strategic comments into greater intimacy with the Father. The three cord strand of worship, word and prayer is always powerful. These will make this small book a big blessing.

The wind of the Spirit is moving in unprecedented ways over the whole of the earth today, breathing life back into dead and dying churches. It is a wind of Spirit-filled, God-centered worship. God the Father is once again being exalted in the fullness of who He is through the undiluted praises of His people. Worship is bringing much needed unity to the body of Christ and is releasing the power of His presence in profound ways - ways that have not been

Worship 101

seen since the early church.

Let *Worship 101* teach you, encourage you and motivate you in your worship of God – and as you do you will be deeply changed. It will light a fire in you that will be seen by all far and wide. Get ready, a revival of worship is coming your way!

> *Pastor Dan Backens*
> *Senior Pastor*
> *New Life Providence Church*
> *Virginia Beach, VA*
> *www.newlifeprovidence.com*

Discovering the God We Worship in 101 Ways

INTRODUCTION

Some years ago, I was deeply touched by the power of the Holy Spirit as He called me to ministry. I was learning to understand God's ways and was experiencing renewed joy as I studied God's word. Sometime soon after, my wife was going to spend a three-day weekend with her sister, and so I thought it would be a good time for me to have a concentrated time alone with God as I sought His direction for my life.

I decided I would go on a three-day total fast. That is, no food, no water, no television, telephone or any other form of media - just me and God. As I launched into the fast, I decided that I would begin with a time of simply worshiping God - not ask for anything.

My heart filled as I began to tell God how much I love Him and appreciate all that he has done for me. I shared with Him everything that came to my mind about His care for me, my destiny, I thanked Him for the call he had upon my life and for everything else I could think of.

I looked at my watch and was surprised when I realized how much time had passed - less than half an hour. Thirty minutes down, seventy-one and a half hours to go.

That is when I realized how little I knew God. I realized I was a stranger to the one I had called Lord for so many years. How was I going to fill the next three days alone with God?

What happened next was the impetus for this book, which you now hold in your hand. I decided I would start by rebuilding my understanding of who God is. I took each phrase that I knew of God and wrote them down, then researched what the Bible said about that phrase. As I continued, the list got longer and longer. It was my first

Worship 101

real lesson in worship - my Worship 101, so to speak.

You have probably read several books on worship. I think that you will immediately notice that this one is a little different. Rather than telling you all I have learned about worship, I will let the word of God do it. This book will also teach you the vocabulary of worship (it will help you to know what to say to God in worship).

Worship 101 is therefore more of a compilation of verses that will help us to discover anew who God is. Each of the 101 expressions herein is based on what the scriptures say about God. For each phrase, there will be a key verse of scripture followed by supporting verses. From time to time, there will be some short notes to help enrich your worship experience and to help create a proper context for your worship experience. However, this has been kept to a minimum in order to keep the focus on the power of the word of God to teach us true worship.

You may read this book in one sitting, but you may get the best mileage if used as a devotional over a period of weeks or months. As you read each phrase, take the time to read each supporting verse and then spend some time meditating on how God is revealing Himself to you. May God bless you as you take this journey.

One of the greatest tragedies of the Christian church today is that it worships a God that it does not know. Yes, we may have Jesus living in our hearts, but who is this Jesus? What are His attributes, His names, His personality traits? And what about God the Father? Do we know who He is? How does He want us to worship Him?

True worship comes when through the power of the Holy Spirit, we bring tribute to God with all our heart, soul and all our mind. Jesus said "God is a Spirit, and they that worship Him must worship Him in spirit and in **truth."**

Discovering the God We Worship in 101 Ways

The Bible tells us who God is, but while we have spent hundreds of dollars on education, church projects and various programs, my guess is that we spend less than 10% of our time and money on learning who our God is and how to worship Him.

Worship 101 seeks to help us understand who God is. This presentation of a combination of 101 names, attributes and characteristics of God are given so that our praise will not be surface praise but will be based on real knowledge of God.

However, while it is important to learn more about the God we worship, knowing about God is not the same as knowing God. It is even more important for us to develop a personal relationship with Him and then to let the praises flow from deep within our souls. Only then does our praise leave the superficial and enter the realm of true worship.

But isn't learning things to say to God during worship very artificial? It can, but it doesn't have to be. Saying a number of phrases and stringing them together is not what worship is all about. True worship comes from the spirit and is blended with our emotions and whole being in sincere reverence and praise to God.

On the other hand, which would you prefer – a person who praises you by saying "You are a great person" or the person who says "I love you because you are a great person with a keen understanding of what it takes to make me feel like a whole person; I also respect you because you are a person of integrity, keen insight and understanding?"

Undoubtedly, if the second person was sincere, you would feel that he/she knows you more and very likely you would prefer it.

While we can never impress God with our words, He loves when we let Him know how much we appreciate

Worship 101

Him and why. Therefore, let us discover together 101 things about our God, which we can use to enhance the worship experience, but remember: True worship comes from deep within.

Discovering the God We Worship in 101 Ways

1

You Are Lord

...And that every tongue should confess that Jesus Christ is Lord to the Glory of God the Father.

Phil. 2: 9-11

Supporting Verses

Zec. 14:9, John 6:68, Rom. 14:9, Rev. 19:6

Worship 101

2

You are the King of Kings

And He has on *His* robe and on His thigh a name written: KING OF KINGS AND LORD OF LORDS.

Rev. 19:16

Supporting Verses

Is. 9:7, Dan. 2:44, Dan. 7:14,
I Cor. 15:24-28

Discovering the God We Worship in 101 Ways

3
You are the Alpha & Omega

"I am the Alpha and the Omega, the Beginning and the End, the First and the Last."

Rev. 22:13

Supporting Verses

Gen. 1:1, Is. 41:4, Is. 43:10, Rev. 1:8, 11

Worship 101

4

Jesus, name above all names

Far above all principality and power and might and dominion, and every name that is named, not only in this age but also in that which is to come.

Ephesians 1:21

Supporting Verses

Luke 1:31-33, Acts 4:12, Phil. 2:10

Discovering the God We Worship in 101 Ways

5

You are my Advocate

(One who pleads our case for us)

My little children, these things I write to you, so that you may not sin. And if anyone sins, we have an Advocate with the Father, Jesus Christ the righteous.

I John 2:1

Supporting Verses

John 14:12&16, Rom. 8:26&27, Heb. 7:25

Worship 101

6

You are Lord of lords

"...and the Lamb will overcome them, for He is Lord of lords and King of kings; and those who are with Him are called chosen and faithful."

Rev. 17:14

Supporting Verses

Deut. 10:17, Neh. 9:6, I Tim. 6:15

Discovering the God We Worship in 101 Ways

7

You are Holy

And one cried to another and said: "Holy, holy, holy is the Lord of hosts; The whole earth is full of His glory!"

Is. 6:3

Supporting Verses

Lev. 11:45, Lev. 19:2, Rev. 4:8, Rev. 15:4

Worship 101

8

Jehovah Tsidkenu

Pronounced—Sid-ken-u
(The Lord our Righteousness)

In His days Judah will be saved and Israel will dwell safely; Now this is His name by which He will be called: The Lord Our Righteousness.

Jer. 23:6

Supporting Verses

Is. 45:24, Rom. 10:4, 2 Cor. 5:21, Titus 3:5

Discovering the God We Worship in 101 Ways

9

You are the Lamb of God

Key Verse — The next day John saw Jesus coming toward him, and said "Behold! The Lamb of God who takes away the sin of the world."

John 1:29

Supporting Verses

Is. 53:7, Acts 8:32, I Peter 1:19, Rev. 13:8

Worship 101

10

You are The Great "I Am"

And God said to Moses, "I Am Who I Am." And He said, "Thus you shall say to the children of Israel, 'I Am has sent me to you.'"

Exodus 3:14

Supporting Verses

John 8:24, Rev. 1:18

Discovering the God We Worship in 101 Ways
GUIDE TO WORSHIP

Why should we tell God things about Himself that He already knows? It is important for us to realize that the worship experience is more than just words. Worship is a way of life. It is living in complete subjection and reverence to God.

The act of expressing our admiration for God, is merely putting into words what we should already be living in our daily lives.

God knows all our thoughts, even before we express them and so it is more important for us to be genuine than to say the things we think God wants to hear.

This does not mean we should not increase our knowledge of who God is. Rather, it means that as we learn more about Him and that knowledge becomes a part of us, we will be able to add richness to the worship experience.

Telling God things about Himself is merely confirming to ourselves what we understand about Him. God does not need our words, but as the verses in this book indicate, He desires it. He wants us to know who He is and it is our words added to our lives of holiness that confirm our knowledge, in the form of worship.

WARNING!!

Worship will usher you into the presence of God but *words can drive you out every time.* There comes a time during the worship experience when in the presence of an awesome God, words are insufficient to express our adoration.

At such times, it is wise to be silent and just gaze at His glory. Even our emotions may fail us at these times.

Worship 101

Sometimes you may cry, sometimes laugh, sometimes you may just look on in wonderment. What is important is for us to know that our *words cannot impress God.* Words are only a tool to help us to get to the place where we may gaze at the manifest presence of a Holy God.

Discovering the God We Worship in 101 Ways

11

You are my Deliverer

 **Key Verse** — And the Lord will deliver me from every evil work and preserve me for His heavenly Kingdom. To Him be glory forever and ever. Amen.

2 Tim. 4:18

Supporting Verses

Ex. 3:8, Ps. 33:19, Acts 7:34

Worship 101

12

You are Mighty God

 Who is this King of glory? The Lord strong and mighty, the Lord mighty in battle.

Ps. 24:8.

Supporting Verses

Prov. 23:11, Luke 1:49-55, Eph. 1:19

Discovering the God We Worship in 101 Ways

13

You are All Powerful
(Omnipotent)

 ...Alleluia! For the Lord God Omnipotent reigns!

Rev. 19:6

Supporting Verses

Job 38:4-11, Ps. 62:11, Rev. 11:15

Worship 101

14

You are All Knowing
(Omniscient)

 ....For the Lord is the God of knowledge; And by Him actions are weighed.

I Sam. 2:36

Supporting Verses

Job 36:4, Ps. 44:21, I John 3:20

Discovering the God We Worship in 101 Ways

15

You are Wonderful

....And His name will be called Wonderful, Counselor, Mighty God, Everlasting Father, Prince of Peace.

Is. 9:6

Supporting Verses

Judges 13:18, Ps. 75:1, Is. 28:29

Worship 101

16

You are my Father

...Our Father in heaven,
Hallowed be Your name.

Matt. 6:9

Supporting Verses

Ps. 68:5, Is. 63:16, 2 Cor. 6:18

Discovering the God We Worship in 101 Ways

17

I bless You

"...Blessing and honor and glory and power be to Him who sits on the throne, and to the Lamb, forever and ever!"

Rev. 5:13b

Supporting Verses

Ps. 103:1&2, Rom. 9:5, Eph. 1:3

Worship 101

18

Jehovah
(Yah, Yahweh)

Behold, God is my salvation, I will trust and not be afraid; for Yah, the Lord, is my strength and song; He also has become my salvation.

Isaiah 12:2

Supporting Verses

Ex. 6:3, Ps. 68:4, Ps. 83:18

Discovering the God We Worship in 101 Ways

19

Immanuel
(God With Us)

"Therefore the Lord Himself will give you a sign: Behold, the virgin shall conceive and bear a son, and shall call His name Immanuel.

Isaiah 7:14

Supporting Verses

Is. 8:8&10, Matt. 1:23, John 1:14

Worship 101

20

El Roi/Rohi
Pronounced—ro-ee'
(The God Who Sees)

Then she called on the name of the LORD who spoke to her, You-Are-the-God-Who-Sees; for she said, "Have I also here seen Him who sees me?"

Gen 16:13

Supporting Verses

2 Chron. 16:9, Ps. 33:13, Zech. 2:8, Song 1:15

Discovering the God We Worship in 101 Ways
EMOTIONS!

Many have wondered what role emotions play in worship. The simple fact is that *worship devoid of emotion is often meaningless.* However, this should come naturally from within – not coerced. Do not worry about outward displays, it is what is in the heart that really matters.

The focus of worship should be God, not to work ourselves into an emotional state. At the same time, stifling heartfelt emotions may be just as bad as attempting to force them.

I grew up in a very rough neighborhood at a time when our community was going through its most violent period in history. I saw things that children should never see and though our family was relatively sheltered from external influences by a very strict mother, internally I became more and more hardened.

At the age of 15, I had a strong confrontation with my mother in which I declared that I had entered into adulthood and had become a man. After that confrontation, I remember making a decision that I would never let anyone see me cry again, and as of that day, I would assume responsibility for all my actions - I was asserting my independence.

With very few exceptions (which I cannot even remember), I think I kept that promise to myself, never to let anyone see me cry. I had made a covenant with myself to become tough inside.

Though I later fell in love with Dahlia and opened my heart to her, and eventually got married in 1987, there was a part of me that remained sheltered and untouchable. That is, until 1997 when my wife helped me to see how much I had allowed my Christian life to drift from the fervor I once had for God.

Worship 101

I was a little surprised when I realized how the seed I had planted in my life some 17 years earlier eventually bore fruit. I went before God and confessed my sins to him, then I prayed a very simple but dangerous prayer: I asked God to change my heart.

Nothing happened immediately (at least nothing I noticed), but a couple weeks later I was in bed sleeping when I suddenly woke up crying. It was strange because I neither had a bad dream nor a nightmare. The Spirit of God had just simply gripped my heart and did something deep inside that changed me forever. That morning in my bed, God called me to ministry. He did it, by first touching my heart - that section deep inside that refused to be touched by emotions.

So how did I do with my promise never to let anyone see me cry again? After that morning, I have failed miserably. Sometimes I will be in a prayer meeting where we are worshiping God and as I enter in fully, I cannot help but weep before God. Those who don't know of my background may think that I am just someone who likes to weep. Oh, they would be so wrong. What has happened is that I have given God permission to let my heart be touched by His Spirit.

There are some who would say they are not emotional people. I can understand that - I have been there. However, the truth is that we are all emotional beings. The issue is that sometimes, we have allowed our emotions to be separated from our spiritual lives. We have been taught it is wrong to be weak or to display emotions or we have determined not to let our emotions become affected by others or circumstances.

Do not shelter your emotions from God; He deserves all of you. Do not work up emotions before God; He deserves to be worshiped in truth.

21

The Amen

(Amen is a Greek word which means "and so let it be." As the Amen, Jesus guarantees God's Promises will be fulfilled)

"And to the angel of the church of the Laodiceans write, these things says the Amen, the Faithful and True Witness, the Beginning of the creation of God."

Rev. 3:14

Supporting Verses

Matt. 24:35, 2 Cor. 1:20, 2 Pet. 3:9

Worship 101

22

You have Divine Power

> **Key Verse:** As His divine power has given to us all things that pertain to life and godliness, through the knowledge of Him who called us by glory and virtue.
>
> 2 Pet. 1:3

Supporting Verses

Ex. 15:6, Nah. 1:3, 1 Pet. 1:5

Discovering the God We Worship in 101 Ways

23

I exalt You

Key Verse

The Lord is my strength and song, and He has become my salvation; He is my God and I will praise Him; my father's God and I will exalt Him.

Exodus 15:2

Supporting Verses

I Chron. 29:11, Ps. 21:13, Ps. 34:3

Worship 101

24

I worship You

Oh come, let us worship and bow down; Let us kneel before the Lord our Maker.

Psalm 95:6

Supporting Verses

John 4:23&24, Rev. 4:10, Rev. 14:7

Discovering the God We Worship in 101 Ways

25

I praise Your name

I will bless the Lord at all times; His praise shall continually be in my mouth.

Psalm 34:1

Supporting Verses

Ps. 33:1, Ps. 147:1, I Cor. 4:5

Worship 101

26

I magnify You

 Oh, magnify the Lord with me, and let us exalt His name together.

Psalm 34:3

Supporting Verses

2 Sam. 7:26, Ps. 35:27, Luke 1: 46

Discovering the God We Worship in 101 Ways

27

You are beautiful in all Your ways

One thing I have desired of the Lord, that will I seek: That I may dwell in the house of the Lord all the days of my life, to behold the beauty of the Lord, and to inquire In His temple.

Psalm 27:4

Supporting Verses

I Chron. 16:29, Ps. 96:9, Is. 33:17

Worship 101

28

Alleluia
(Praise the Lord)

After these things I heard a loud voice of a great multitude in heaven, saying, "Alleluia! Salvation and glory and honor and power belong to the Lord our God."

Revelation 19:1

Supporting Verses

Ps. 113:1&2, Ps. 117, Rev. 19:3, 4&6

Discovering the God We Worship in 101 Ways

29

I extol Your Name

Sing to God, Sing praises to His name; Extol Him who rides on the clouds, by His name Yah, and rejoice before Him.

Psalm 68:4

Supporting Verses

Ps. 30:1, Ps. 145:1, Is. 52:13

Worship 101

30

You are high and lifted up

...I saw the Lord sitting on a throne, high and lifted up, and the train of His robe filled the temple.

Isaiah 6:1

Supporting Verses

Acts 2:33, Acts 5:31, Phil. 2:9

Discovering the God We Worship in 101 Ways
IDEAS FOR FAMILY WORSHIP

One of the ways you can draw your family closer is through family worship. This is a special time you and your family should set aside on a regular basis to worship God.

Consistency is the key. It is better to do it once every week than three times in one week and then not do it for another month.

Here are some suggestions to help you in this important area of family life:

First, sing together – no matter what type of singing voice each member of the family has. Remember, the focus should be on God, not talent. Sometimes, however, if no one is able to play an instrument or if there are no good singers in the family, you may want to sing along with a worship CD. Choose the songs beforehand. If the songs are not known by each member of the family, try to get the words, either from the CD jacket or if you are computer savvy, you may even download the words online.

Second, have a time of one sentence prayers of thanksgiving and adoration. Here each person gets to pray in turn a number of times rather than one person always praying. Also, hold hands while praying. This may be strange at first, but you will soon get accustomed to it.

Next, read the Word of God together. You may read alternate verses or take turns reading at different times.

If your family has never worshiped together, don't start by announcing that everyone will meet at a certain time. Instead, you begin to have your personal time of worship then gradually invite others to join in.

Worship 101

31

Jehovah Jireh
(The Lord Will Provide)

And my God shall supply all your need according to His riches in glory by Christ Jesus.

Philippians 4:19

Supporting Verses

Gen. 22:14, Is. 58:11, Jer. 31:12-14

Discovering the God We Worship in 101 Ways

32

You are Almighty God
(El Shaddai)

When Abram was ninety-nine years old, the Lord appeared to Abram and said to him, "I am Almighty God; walk before Me and be blameless."

Genesis 17:1

Supporting Verses

Ex. 6:2&3, Ps. 91:1, Rev. 11:17

Worship 101

33

There is none above You

> ...One God and Father of all, who is above all, and through all, and in you all.
>
> Ephesians 4:6

Key Verse

Supporting Verses

Eph. 1:20-22, Heb. 7:26

Discovering the God We Worship in 101 Ways

34

There is none like unto You

Who is like You, O Lord, among the gods? Who is like You, Glorious in holiness, Fearful in praises, doing wonders?

Exodus 15:11

Supporting Verses

Deut. 33:29, 2 Sam. 7:22, I Kings 8:23

Worship 101

35

You are the Righteous Judge

Finally, there is laid up for me the crown of righteousness, which the Lord the Righteous Judge will give to me on that day, and not to me only but also to all who have loved His appearing.

2 Timothy 4:8

Supporting Verses

Deut. 32:36, John 5:30, Rev. 19:2

Discovering the God We Worship in 101 Ways

36

You are my Defender

But let all those rejoice who put their trust in You; Let them ever shout for joy, because You defend them; Let those also who love Your name be joyful in You.

Psalm 5:11

Supporting Verses

Ps. 82:3, Ps. 94:22, Zech. 9:15

Worship 101

37

You are my strength

Key Verse: The Lord is my strength and my shield; My heart trusted in Him, and I am helped; Therefore my heart greatly rejoices, and with my song I will praise Him.

Psalm 28:7

Supporting Verses

2 Sam. 22:3, Ps. 118:14, Is. 12:2

Discovering the God We Worship in 101 Ways

38

You are my refuge

The eternal God is your refuge, and underneath are the everlasting arms; He will thrust out the enemy from before you, and will say, "Destroy!"

Deuteronomy 33:27

Supporting Verses

Ps. 9:9, Ps. 46:1, Ps. 59:16

Worship 101

39

Abba, Father
(Intimate Aramaic for father)

Key Verse

For you did not receive the spirit of bondage again to fear, but you received the spirit of adoption by whom we cry out, "Abba Father."

Romans 8:15

Supporting Verses

Mark 14:36, Galatians 4:6

Discovering the God We Worship in 101 Ways

40

You are my hiding place

You are my hiding place; You shall preserve me from trouble; You shall surround me with songs of deliverance.

Psalm 32:7

Supporting Verses

Deut. 33:12, Ps. 17:8, Ps. 119:114

Worship 101
THE BIBLICAL NAMES FOR GOD

In the Bible there are many names for God. In the Old Testament, the sacred Hebrew name for God is YHWH. Vowels were not used and the Jews avoided every mention of the name because they believed it was a capital offence, which was punishable by death (Lev. 24:16).

Later, the vowels "a" and "e" were added by scholars who translated the name into English as Yahweh or Jehovah (shortened form – Yah or Jah) which designates God's nature in relation to man. He is a personal Holy Being and a Spirit.

A very popular term for God in the Old Testament is El. This term is used in reference to both the God of Israel as well as pagan deities. The plural "Elohim" is used by many Old Testament writers with singular verbs and adjectives to talk about a singular God.

In the New Testament, the Greek Word "Theos" takes the place of El, Elohim and Elyon (the Most High).

In the copying of New Testament manuscripts in the original Greek, the most common mistake was replacing "Theos" (God) with "Kurios" (Lord). Whenever translators noticed this difference in manuscripts, they inserted "Lord God."

Discovering the God We Worship in 101 Ways

41

You are my shield

After these things the Word of the Lord came to Abram in a vision, saying, "Do not be afraid, Abram, I am your shield, your exceedingly great reward."

Genesis 15:1

Supporting Verses

Ps. 33:20, Ps. 59:11, 2 Sam. 22:31

Worship 101

42

You are the River of Life

But whoever drinks of the water that I shall give him will never thirst. But the water that I shall give him will become in him a fountain of water springing up into everlasting life.

John 4:14

Supporting Verses

Ps. 36:8, Ezek. 47:1-12, Rev. 22:1

Discovering the God We Worship in 101 Ways

43

My Savior

And we have seen and testify that the Father has sent the Son as Savior of the world.

I John 4:14

Supporting Verses

Is. 43:11, Luke 2:11, Acts 5:31

Worship 101

44

You are the All Sufficient One

Key Verse — Not that we are sufficient of ourselves to think of anything as being from ourselves, but our sufficiency is from God.

2 Corinthians 3:5

Supporting Verses

Ps. 55:22, Ps 81:10, 2 Cor. 9:8

Discovering the God We Worship in 101 Ways

45

You are unchanging
(Immutable)

Key Verse

Jesus Christ is the same yesterday, today and forever.

Hebrews 13:8

Supporting Verses

Ps. 102:25-27, Mal 3:6, John 8:58, Heb. 1:12

Worship 101

46

Anointed One
(Christ – Messiah)

"The Spirit of the Lord is upon Me, because He has anointed Me to preach the gospel to the poor..."

Luke 4:18

Supporting Verses

John 1:41, Acts 4:27, Acts 10:38

Discovering the God We Worship in 101 Ways

47

Adonai
(Supreme Lord and Master)

And He is the head of the body, the church, who is the beginning, the firstborn from the dead, that in all things He may have the preeminence.

Colossians 1:18

Supporting Verses

Ps. 2, Is. 6:1-5

Worship 101

48

The Lord is Good

Key Verse: Oh give thanks to the Lord, for He is good! For His mercy endures forever.

Psalm 107:1

Supporting Verses

Ps. 25:8, Ps. 31:19, Matt. 19:17, Luke 18:19

Discovering the God We Worship in 101 Ways

49

You are my Redeemer

For I know that my Redeemer lives, and He shall stand at last on the earth.

Job 19:25

Supporting Verses

Is. 49:26, Is. 44:24, Is. 60:16

Worship 101

50

You are my Comforter/ Helper

Blessed be the God and Father of our Lord Jesus Christ, the Father of mercies and God of all comfort...

2 Corinthians 1:3

Supporting Verses

Ps. 10:14, John 14:26, John 16:7, Heb. 13:6

Discovering the God We Worship in 101 Ways
WHAT IS YOUR WORSHIP RATIO?

Have you ever stopped to think that in the Bible, there are many more calls to worship than calls for us to pray about our needs? In the books of Psalm and Revelation, for example, while prayers of supplication are important, worship plays a greater role.

So how is your prayer life? Is it balanced or do you forget to spend time in worship? If so, begin by setting aside a time when you will talk to God but will not ask Him for anything. Instead, tell Him how much you admire Him and praise Him for who He is and all the things that He has done.

If you have never done this before, it may feel strange at first. After all, many people think of God only as a person who we pray to about our needs. Now as you worship, you will begin to see God in a new light.

This does not mean that God is changing, what it means is that you are beginning to be conformed to His image. That is one of the powers of worship, it changes us in the presence of an unchanging God.

Practice doing this everyday, you will find that the more you worship, the less likely you are to live an unholy life. Why? Because we become more and more like the object of our worship. The more time we spend learning about God, looking at the things we like about Him and rehearsing his characteristics, the more we take on His personality traits.

Researchers in the field of media effects have studied the phenomenon in which people take on characteristics of the ones they worship and they even have a name for it; they call it "identification." What they have discovered is that fans of a television program become "vicariously involved" with characters on these programs. In other words

Worship 101

the fans adopt the values and behaviors of the celebrities they admire. Media effects researchers have found that media consumers become involved with characters (very often music celebrities) due to repeated exposure to their work.

In the same way, the more we expose ourselves to God and begin to enjoy Him for who He is, the more we will naturally take on His characteristics—we identify with Him. The Bible puts it this way:

> *But we all, with unveiled face, beholding as in a mirror the Glory of the Lord, are being transformed into the same image from glory to glory, just as by the Spirit of the Lord.*
> 2 Corinthians 3:18

While having our needs met through prayer will help us to have more confidence in God's love for us, seeking God to do things for us or for others does not have the power to change us to the same extent that worshiping God does—so what's your worship ratio?

Discovering the God We Worship in 101 Ways

51

The Lord Most High
(Jehovah Elyon)

Key Verse

I will praise the Lord according to His righteousness, and will sing praise to the name of the Lord Most High.

Psalm 7:17

Supporting Verses

Ps. 47:2, Ps. 91:1, Dan. 4:17

Worship 101

52

You are my Salvation

The Lord is my strength and my song, and He has become my salvation.

Psalm 118:14

Supporting Verses

Ps. 85:9, Ps. 98:3, Is. 12:2

Discovering the God We Worship in 101 Ways

53

Jehovah Shammah
(The Lord is Present)

God is our refuge and strength, a very present help in trouble.

Psalm 46:1

Supporting Verses

Gen. 28:15, Deut. 31:6, Ezek. 48:35

Worship 101

54

Merciful God

But God who is rich in mercy, because of His great love with which He loved us, even when we were dead in trespasses, made us alive together with Christ (by grace you have been saved).

Ephesians 2:4&5

Supporting Verses

Num. 14:18, I Chron. 16:34, Ps. 103:17, Dan. 9:9

Discovering the God We Worship in 101 Ways

55

Jehovah Sabaoth

(Lord of Hosts – commander of the armies of heaven)

Key Verse

And as Isaiah said before: Unless the Lord of Sabaoth had left us a seed, we would have become like Sodom, and we would have been made like Gomorrah.

Romans 9:29

Supporting Verses

Josh. 5:14, I Sam. 17:45&50, James 5:4

Worship 101

56

Your love is unfailing

Key Verse

The Lord has appeared of old to me saying: "Yes, I have loved you with an everlasting love; therefore with loving-kindness I have drawn you."

Jeremiah 31:3

Supporting Verses

John 3:16, John 15:12&13, Rom. 8:35-39, I John 3:16

Discovering the God We Worship in 101 Ways

57

You are my High Priest

For we do not have a High Priest who cannot sympathize with our weaknesses, but was in all points tempted as we are, yet without sin.

Hebrews 4:15

Supporting Verses

Ps. 110:4, Heb. 2:17, Heb. 5:6

Worship 101

58

My Husband

For your Maker is your husband, the Lord of hosts is His name; and your Redeemer is the Holy One of Israel; He is called the God of the whole earth.

Isaiah 54:5

Supporting Verses

Jer. 3:14&15, Hosea 2:7, 19&20, Rev. 19:7

Discovering the God We Worship in 101 Ways

59

Refiner's Fire

Key Verse — Behold I have refined you, but not as silver; I have tested you in the furnace of affliction.

Isaiah 48:10

Supporting Verses

Job 23:10, Mal. 3:2&3, I Cor. 3:11-15

Worship 101

60

My Maker

In that day a man will look to his Maker and his eyes will have respect for the Holy One of Israel.

Isaiah 17:7

Supporting Verses

Gen 1:26&27, Job 35:10, Job 36:3, Rev. 4:9-11

Discovering the God We Worship in 101 Ways
THE FIRST COMMANDMENT

We are already well past the half way mark in our journey to discover the God we worship. If you have made it this far, chances are you are a worshiper, not because it is a good Christian discipline, but because you enjoy worshiping God. We don't worship because we have to, we worship because we may—and we have found that there is joy in the presence of God as we worship.

Now it is time to take our devotion to God to the next level. Where should we turn when it is time to take our worship to the ultimate level? The Bible of course.

Matthew 22: 35-40
> *³⁵Then one of them, a lawyer, asked Him a question, testing Him, and saying, ³⁶"Teacher, which is the great commandment in the law?" ³⁷Jesus said to Him, "'You shall love the Lord your God with **all your h**eart, with **all your soul**, and with **all your mind**.' ³⁸"**This is the first and great commandment**. ³⁹"And the second is like it: 'You shall love your neighbor as yourself.' ⁴⁰"On these two commandments hang all the Law and the prophets."*

Want to take your worship to the ultimate level? It is not in going forward - it is in going backward to take care of the first thing first: Learning to love God with "all your heart," "all your soul" and "all your mind." There is no room for double-mindedness - it is giving God our ALL.

I confess that I don't think that I am there as yet. The cares of the world sometimes get the better of me and I find that my love for God is not as pure as the first commandment requires. So how do we get there from here?

Worship 101

I believe the first step is to admit our shortcomings before God. However, confessing our shortfalls is only the first step; this must be followed by a daily decision to make God the priority in our lives.

That is not the same thing as saying that the first thing you should do each day is spend time with God. That is important, but making God priority goes beyond that. It means He should come first when I am walking up the stairs, when someone cuts me off in traffic, when I am late for an appointment, when I am upset with my neighbor…

Here is a big one—God needs to be priority in my life when I am too busy to make Him priority. How do you do that? You need to endeavor to always be in an attitude of worship. "Therefore, whether you eat or drink, or whatever you do, do all to the glory of God" (1 Cor. 10: 31).

Now don't get ahead of yourself; always being in an attitude of worship does not mean being spooky. It does not mean always speaking in "Christian jargoneese," nor does it mean you can no longer have fun. What it means is that in everything you do, you want the light of God to shine through you. Living a life of integrity that attracts people to God every day and in everything you do is an act of worship and devotion to God.

Don't zone out on others—give them your full attention when you are with them, just as you would like God to give His full attention to you when you are with Him. When you reflect God in all you do, you worship Him with your whole life.

Work hard, play hard, laugh heartily, cry deeply, think creatively, act shrewdly, but in all things let your life reflect the one who is most beautiful, wonderful, caring, your strong tower, your Jehovah Jireh, all sufficient, patient, kind, loving, etc.

Discovering the God We Worship in 101 Ways

61

My Friend

Greater love has no one than this, than to lay down one's life for his friends.

John 15:13

Supporting Verses

Prov. 17:17, Luke 12:4, John 15:14

Worship 101

62

You are the Ancient of Days

Key Verse

I watched till thrones were put in place, and the Ancient of Days was seated; His garment was white as snow, and the hair of His head was like pure wool.

Daniel 7:9

Supporting Verses

Job 36:26, Ps. 90:2, Rev. 1:17&18

Discovering the God We Worship in 101 Ways

63

The Creator

Key Verse

Have you not known? Have you not heard? The everlasting God, the Lord, the Creator of the ends of the earth, neither faints nor is weary. His understanding is unsearchable.

Isaiah 40:28

Supporting Verses

Gen. 1:1, Col. 1:16, Rev. 4:11

Worship 101

64

Prince of Peace

For unto us a Child is born, unto us a Son is given; And the government will be upon His shoulder. And His name will be called Wonderful, Counselor, Mighty God, Everlasting Father, Prince of Peace.

Isaiah 9:6

Supporting Verses

Is. 26:3, Hagg. 2:9, Eph. 2:14-16

Discovering the God We Worship in 101 Ways

65

You are able

Now to Him who is able to keep you from stumbling, and to present you faultless before the presence of His glory with exceeding joy...

Jude 24

Supporting Verses

Phil, 3:21, Heb. 7:25, Rev. 5:3-5

Worship 101

66

You are Lily of the valleys

I am the rose of Sharon, and the lily of the valleys.

Song. 2:1

Supporting Verse

Ps. 23:4

Discovering the God We Worship in 101 Ways

67

You are the way

Jesus said to him, "I am the way, the truth and the life. No one comes to the Father except through Me.

John 14:6

Supporting Verses

John 10:9&10, Eph. 2:18, Heb. 10:20

Worship 101

68

The Word

In the beginning was the
Word, and the Word was
with God, and
the Word was God.

John 1:1

Supporting Verses

John 1:14, Heb. 6:5, Rev. 19:13

Discovering the God We Worship in 101 Ways

69

Lion of the tribe of Judah

But one of the elders said to me, "Do not weep. Behold, the Lion of the tribe of Judah, the Root of David, has prevailed to open the scroll and to loose its seven seals."

Revelation 5:5

Supporting Verses

Gen. 49:9&10, Hos. 5:14&15, Heb. 7:14-16

Worship 101

70

The Bread of Life

Key Verse

And Jesus said to them, "I am the bread of life. He who comes to Me shall never hunger, and he who believes in Me shall never thirst."

John 6:35

Supporting Verses

Matt. 26:26, John 6:48, I Cor. 10:16

LOVE LETTER FROM GOD

My Beloved Friend,

It's been a long time since you have been on my mind. I have loved you from the very beginning and I still love you now.

I know sometimes it is difficult for you to understand why I love you so much. I know it is sometimes just as difficult for you to understand why it is my desire for you to love me so much.

I love when you talk to me and let me know how much you appreciate me. I love when you think of me and can hardly wait to be with me again. I love when you smile at me and when your thoughts turn toward me. My eyes are also upon you and when our eyes meet, it gives me special pleasure.

I like to hear your voice but even more, I love to hear your heart beat for me. I love it when you come and sit by me even when you have nothing much to say.

I know you don't understand how deep, how high or how wide my love is for you. My love for you is unconditional and unending—I would love you even if you didn't love me back—but I can't help being happy that you love me too.

Yours forever,

I AM

Worship 101

71

The Good Shepherd
**(Jehovah Raah)
- pronounced raw-ah**

"I am the good shepherd; and I know My sheep, and am known by My own."

John 10:14

Supporting Verses

Ps. 23:1, John 10:11, Heb. 13:20-21, I Pet. 5:4

Discovering the God We Worship in 101 Ways

72

Immortal One

Who alone has immortality, dwelling in unapproachable light, whom no man has seen or can see, to whom be honor and everlasting power. Amen.

I Timothy 6:16

Supporting Verses

I Cor. 15:53-57, I Tim. 1:17, 2 Tim. 1:10

Worship 101

73

Light of the world

Then Jesus spoke to them again, saying, "I am the light of the world. He who follows Me shall not walk in darkness, but have the light of life."

John 8:12

Supporting Verses

Ps. 27:1, Mic. 7:8, John 1:4, John 12, 46

Discovering the God We Worship in 101 Ways

74

You are my shelter

...But the Lord will be a shelter for His people, and the strength of the children of Israel.

Joel 3:16b

Supporting Verses

Deut. 33:12, Ps. 61:4, Ps. 143:9

Worship 101

75

You are Worthy

"You are worthy, O Lord, to receive glory and honor and power; For You created all things, and by Your will they exist and were created."

Rev. 4:11

Supporting Verses

2 Sam. 22:4, Ps. 18:3, Rev. 5:9&12

Discovering the God We Worship in 101 Ways

76

You are my Healer
(Jehovah Rapha)

But He was wounded for our transgressions, He was bruised for our iniquities; The chastisement for our peace was upon Him, and by His stripes we are healed.

Isaiah 53:5

Supporting Verses

Ex. 15:26, Deut. 32:39, 1 Pet. 2:24

Worship 101

77

You are everywhere
(Omnipresent)

Where can I go from Your Spirit? O where can I flee from Your presence? If I ascend into heaven, You are there...

Psalm 139:7-10

Supporting Verses

2 Chron. 16:9, Jer. 23:23&24, Heb. 13:5

Discovering the God We Worship in 101 Ways

78

You are the Rose of Sharon

 I am the rose of Sharon, and the lily of the valleys.

Song. 2:1

Supporting Verses

Is. 35:1&2, Is. 65:9&10 (prophecy)

Worship 101

79

Teacher
(Rabboni)

"You call Me Teacher and Lord, and you say well, for so I am."

John 13:13

Supporting Verses

Matt. 23:8&10, John 14:26, John 20:16

Discovering the God We Worship in 101 Ways

80

Author and finisher of our faith

Key Verse — Looking unto Jesus, the author and finisher of our faith, who for the joy that was set before Him endured the cross, despising the shame, and has sat down at the right hand of the throne of God.

Hebrews 12:2

Supporting Verses

1 John 1:1-3, Jude 24&25, Rev. 1:4-6

Worship 101

THE RELEVANCE OF THE OLD TESTAMENT NAMES OF GOD

Some time ago I heard someone say that they never ever refer to God by any of the names used in the Old Testament. Their reasoning was that the names for God used in the Old Testament were names used that indicated how those people knew God at the time and shouldn't be used by us today.

I didn't give much thought to what the person said, as I felt it was merely one person's opinion. However, much more recently, I heard a very well known and respected speaker dismiss the present day use of the names of God as used in the Old Testament. The speaker went as far as to say that the use of names such as *Jehovah Nissi*, is a sign of an "orphan spirit," similar to the orphan spirit of the children of Israel who did not know God as "Father."

I do not agree with this teaching and I feel it goes beyond what the scripture teaches. The Bible teaches that:

All scripture is given by the inspiration of God, and is profitable for doctrine, for reproof, for correction, for instruction in righteousness, that the man of God may be complete, thoroughly equipped for every good work.

(2 Timothy 3:16&17).

The revelation of God to His people in the Old Testament is still relevant to us today. It helps us to understand who our God is and it adds to our appreciation of His work among His people. Gaining a deeper understanding of the different characteristics or traits of God in no way detracts from our understanding of Him in any other way.

I applaud those who have gained a deep revelation of God in a particular area, but let us never attempt to limit our limitless God. He is "All That" and more.

Discovering the God We Worship in 101 Ways

81

Chief Cornerstone

Therefore, to you who believe, He is precious; but to those who are disobedient, "The stone which the builders rejected has become the chief cornerstone."

1 Peter 2:7

Supporting Verses

Ps. 118:22, Matt. 21:42-44, Luke 20:17&18, Eph. 2:20

Worship 101

82

Heir of all things

...has in these last days spoken to us by His Son, whom He has appointed heir of all things, through whom also He made the worlds.

Hebrews 1:2

Supporting Verses

Rom. 8:17, Zech. 2:12, Rev. 5:11-13

Discovering the God We Worship in 101 Ways

83

Horn of salvation

(Horn represents strength and power)

And has raised up a horn of salvation for us in the house of His servant David.

Luke 1:69

Supporting Verses

1 Sam. 2:10, Ps. 18:2, Ezek. 29:21

Worship 101

84

Resurrection and Life

Jesus said to her, "I am the resurrection and the life. He who believes in Me, though he may die, he shall live."

John 11:25

Supporting Verses

John 5:21, Heb. 2:14&15, Rev. 1:18

Discovering the God We Worship in 101 Ways

85

Jehovah Nissi
("The Lord Our Banner" – a standard or flag raised high, around which people may rally)

And Moses built an altar and called its name "The Lord is My Banner."

Exodus 17:15

Supporting Verses

John 3:14&15, Heb. 12:2, Phil. 3:12-14

Worship 101

86

Jehovah Shalom
(The Lord Our Peace)

Key Verse

So Gideon built an altar there to the Lord and called it "The Lord is Peace."

Judges 6:24

Supporting Verses

John 14:27, Rom. 5:1, 2 Thess. 3:16

Discovering the God We Worship in 101 Ways

87

Living God

And Joshua said, "By this you shall know that the living God is among you, and that He will without fail drive out from before you the Canaanites and the Hittites and the Hivites and the Perizzites and the Girgashites and the Amorites and the Jebusites."

Joshua 3:10

Supporting Verses

Matt. 28:5-7, 1 Cor. 15:3-8, Rev. 1:18

Worship 101

88

You are my Rock

The Lord lives! Blessed be my Rock, let God be exalted, the Rock of My Salvation.

2 Samuel 22:47

Supporting Verses

Ps. 18:46, Ps. 31:3, 1 Cor. 10:4

Discovering the God We Worship in 101 Ways

89

Protector

Key Verse

No evil shall befall you, nor shall any plague come near your dwelling. For He shall give His angels charge over you, to keep you in all your ways.

Psalm 91:10&11

Supporting Verses

Ps. 119:117, John 10:27-30, Jude 24

Worship 101

90

Fire of God

For our God is a consuming fire.

Heb. 12:29

Supporting Verses

Ex. 24:17, 1 Kings 18:24, 36-39, Matt. 3:11

Discovering the God We Worship in 101 Ways
MUSIC AND WORSHIP

Traditionally, when someone mentions the word *worship*, many people automatically think about worship as it relates to singing. As a non-musician, I have chosen to stay away from the musical aspects of worship, as there are many people who can do a far better job at discussing music and worship than I could ever do.

However, as we come towards the end of our journey together, it is important to acknowledge that music with worship is a very powerful combination. Music adds joy to worship and helps us remember spiritual truths and scriptures that we wouldn't normally be able to. Music has a way of transcending our logical thinking and taking us to a place where we worship more from our spirits than from our minds.

In the congregation where I worship, we have different forms of worship and prayer, many of them incorporating music. Our prayer meetings, for example, range from meetings in which everyone remains silent as music is played, to meetings in which we sing our prayers from the scriptures. In our *International Café Service* at our church, we often worship in up to about ten different languages. Though the only words I know in some languages are the words of worship we sing, there is a sense of wonder and joy that I experience while joining my brothers and sisters of different cultures and tongues to worship.

Music therefore is important in worship both on an individual and corporate level. If you are a musician, I encourage you to make melodies to God during worship. If on the other hand, you are like me, I encourage you to make a joyful noise unto the Lord and come before His presence with singing (Psalm 100:1&2).

Worship 101

91

Spirit of Truth

"However, when He, the Spirit of truth, has come, He will guide you into all truth; for he will not speak on His own authority, but whatever He hears He will speak; and He will tell you things to come."

John 16:13

Supporting Verses

Deut. 32:4, John 18:37, 1 John 5:6

Discovering the God We Worship in 101 Ways

92

I adore You
(To worship with profound reverence; to pay divine honors to)

Oh come, let us worship and bow down; Let us kneel before the Lord our Maker. For He is our God, and we are the people of His pasture, the sheep of His hand.

Psalm 95:6&7

Supporting Verses

Ps. 68:35, Ps. 139:14, Dan. 4:3

Worship 101

93

I love You

We love Him because
He first loved us.

1 John 4:19

Supporting Verses

Deut. 6:5, Ps. 31:23, Song 2:4, Rom. 5:5

Discovering the God We Worship in 101 Ways

94

Glory be to You, O God

You are worthy, O Lord, to receive glory and honor and power; for You created all things and by Your will they exist and were created.

Rev. 4:11

Supporting Verses

Luke 2:14, Rom. 16:27, 1 Peter 4:11

Worship 101

95

Breath/Wind of God

(The Hebrew & Greek words for Spirit are also translated Breath and Wind)

God is Spirit, and those who worship Him must worship in Spirit and truth.

John 4:24

Supporting Verses

Ps. 143:10, Ezek, 37:14, Acts 2:1-4

Discovering the God We Worship in 101 Ways

96

You are the Great Physician

Bless the Lord, O my soul and forget not all His benefits: Who forgives all your iniquities, who heals all your diseases.

Psalm 103:2&3

Supporting Verses

Matt. 4:23, Matt. 9:12&13, Luke 8:43&44

Worship 101

97

You are my fortress

 The Lord is my rock and my fortress and my deliverer; My God, my strength, in whom I will trust; My shield and the horn of my salvation, my stronghold.

Psalm 18:2

Supporting Verses

Ps. 91:2, Ps. 125:2, Jer. 16:19

Discovering the God We Worship in 101 Ways

98

You are my portion

"The Lord is my portion," says my soul, "therefore I hope in Him!"

Lamentations 3:24

Supporting Verses

Ps. 16:5, Ps. 73:26, Eph. 1:11

Worship 101

99

You are a covenant keeping God

My covenant I will not break, nor alter the word that has gone out of my lips.

Psalm 89:34

Supporting Verses

Num. 23:19, Ps. 119:89, Heb. 13:20&21

Discovering the God We Worship in 101 Ways

100

Jehovah M'Keddesh
(The Lord my sanctifier)

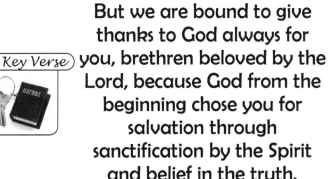

But we are bound to give thanks to God always for you, brethren beloved by the Lord, because God from the beginning chose you for salvation through sanctification by the Spirit and belief in the truth.

2 Thessalonians 2:13

Supporting Verses

John 17:19, 1 Cor. 6:11, Eph. 5:26&27

Worship 101

101

Your name is Jesus

(Literally "Savior" – Jehovah is Salvation)

And she will bring forth a Son and you shall call His name Jesus, for He will save His people from their sins."

Matthew 1:21

Supporting Verses

Luke 1:31, Luke 2:21, Acts 4:12, Rev. 22:20

FINAL WORDS

Isn't our God great and big and marvelous? No doubt, as you have reviewed the pages of this book, you have thought of a number of names and characteristics of God found in the Bible, that are not included.

The aim of this book was not to give a complete list but rather to help you on your journey towards intimacy with God. We know God as our Kinsman Redeemer, the Faithful God, Possessor of Heaven & Earth, the Beautiful Bridegroom, the God who forgives, God our exceeding Joy, Revealer of Mysteries, the Self-Existing One, the Lord who is Faithful, a defense for the helpless, the Everlasting Arms, the One who lifts my head, the Fairest of Ten Thousand, the Hope of Israel, our Liberty, our Rewarder, the Coming King and the list goes on...

May God continue to draw you closer to Himself as you worship Him in spirit and in truth.

INDEX

Abba, Father	44
Adonai (Supreme Lord and Master)	53
Advocate	5
All Knowing (Omniscient)	16
All Powerful (Omnipotent)	15
All Sufficient One	50
Alleluia (Praise the Lord)	32
Almighty God (El Shaddai)	37
Alpha & Omega	3
Ancient of Days	72
Anointed One	52
Author and finisher of our faith	91
Beautiful in all Your ways	31
Bread of Life	80
Breath/Wind of God	108
Chief Cornerstone	93
Comforter/Helper	56
Covenant keeping God	112
Defender	41
Deliverer	13
Divine Power	26
El Roi/Rohi	22
El Shaddai	37
Everywhere (Omnipresent)	88
Father	18
Fire of God	102
Fortress	110
Friend	71
Glory be to You, O God	107
God With Us	21
Good Shepherd (Jehovah Raah)	82

INDEX

Great "I Am"	10
Great Physician	109
Healer (Jehovah Rapha)	87
Heir of all things	94
Helper	56
Hiding place	45
High and lifted up	34
High Priest	65
Holy	7
Horn of salvation	95
Husband	66
I adore You	105
I bless You	19
I exalt You	27
I extol Your Name	33
I love You	106
I magnify You	30
I praise Your Name	29
I worship You	28
Immanuel (God With US)	21
Immortal One	83
Immutable	51
Jehovah (Yah, Yahweh)	20
Jehovah Elyon (The Lord Most High)	59
Jehovah Jireh (The Lord Will Provide)	36
Jehovah M'Keddesh (The Lord My Sanctifier)	113
Jehovah Nissi (The Lord our Banner)	97
Jehovah Raah (The Good Shepherd)	82
Jehovah Rapha (The Lord our Healer)	87
Jehovah Sabaoth (Lord of Hosts)	63
Jehovah Shalom (The Lord our Peace)	98

INDEX

Jehovah Shammah (The Lord is Present)	61
Jehovah Tsidkenu (The Lord our Righteousness)	8
Jesus, name above all names	4
King of Kings	2
Lamb of God	9
Light of the world	84
Lily of the valleys	76
Lion of the tribe of Judah	79
Living God	99
Lord	1
Lord Most High (Jehovah Elyon)	59
Lord of lords	6
Maker	68
Merciful God	62
Mighty God	14
Omnipotent	15
Omniscient	16
Portion	111
Praise the Lord	32
Prince of Peace	74
Protector	101
Rabboni	90
Redeemer	55
Refiner's Fire	67
Refuge	43
Resurrection and Life	96
Righteous Judge	40
River of Life	48
Rock	100
Rose of Sharon	89
Salvation	60

INDEX

Savior	49
Shelter	85
Shield	47
Spirit of Truth	104
Strength	42
Supreme Lord and Master	53
Teacher (Rabboni)	90
The Amen	25
The Creator	73
The Lord is Good	54
The Way	77
The Word	78
There is none above You	38
There is none like unto You	39
Unchanging (immutable)	51
Wind of God	108
Wonderful	17
Worthy	86
Yah, Yahweh	20
You are able	75
Your love is unfailing	64
Your Name is Jesus	114

To invite Dr. Chris Cunningham to speak at your conference or ministry, please contact him through his website: FireWorks International
www.fireworkstv.com

Sample topics: * *Worship* * *Evangelism* * *Growing in the supernatural* * *Normal supernatural Christianity* * *Travailing prayers and the heart cry of the Spirit* * *Prayer and intercession* * *Perseverance in prayer* * *How to develop an effective Prayer Ministry (leadership training)* * *Altar ministry that breaks the chain (leadership training)*.

Made in the USA
Charleston, SC
16 May 2010